MW01014232

cooking the

IRISH way

Chicken and leek pie (recipe on page 33) is a rich, savory dish that is perfect when accompanied by chicory salad with tangy buttermilk-egg dressing (recipe on page 43).

cooking the
IRISH way

HELGA HUGHES

PHOTOGRAPHS BY ROBERT L. AND DIANE WOLFE

easy menu
ethnic
cookbooks

Lerner Publications Company ∎ Minneapolis

Editor: Rebecca McKay

Additional photographs courtesy of the Irish Tourist Board, pp. 7,
11, 13, 14; Christabel D. Grant, p. 9; Edward Smith, p. 10. Border,
map, and illustrations on pp. 17, 29, 39 by Laura Westlund.

Library of Congress Cataloging-in-Publication Data

Hughes, Helga.
    Cooking the Irish way / Helga Hughes ; photographs by
Robert L. and Diane Wolfe.
        p.   cm. — (Easy menu ethnic cookbooks)
    Includes index.
    Summary: A simple introduction to Ireland, presenting some
traditional recipes such as soda bread, Irish stew, Dublin coddle,
and champ.
    ISBN 0-8225-0931-8 (alk. paper)
    1. Cookery, Irish—Juvenile literature. 2. Ireland—Social life
and customs—Juvenile literature. [1. Cookery, Irish.
2. Ireland—Social life and customs.] I. Wolfe, Robert L. ill.
II. Wolfe, Diane, ill. III. Title. IV. Series.
TX717.5.H84 1996
641.59415—dc20   95–49892

Manufactured in the United States of America
1 2 3 4 5 6 – JR – 00 99 98 97 96

**Peppery watercress, potatoes, and cream make
a nutritious soup that can be served hot or cold.
(Recipe is on page 32.)**

CONTENTS

Flag of Ireland

Potatoes

Fish

NORTHERN IRELAND

NORTH ATLANTIC OCEAN

Dairy Cattle

Wheat

Beef Cattle

Hogs

Beef Cattle

IRISH SEA

Beef Cattle

Oats

Barley

C E N T R A L   P L A I N

Dairy Products

Fish

Potatoes

Dublin

Salmon

River

Barley

Potatoes

Seafood

Beef Cattle

Sugar Beets

Salmon

Shannon

Hills and Mountains

Farming and Stock Raising

Sheep

Poultry

Forestry

Sheep

Seafood

Seafood

Forestry

I R E L A N D

INTRODUCTION

"Follow steadfastly to the ways of your ancestors."

—Irish proverb

By making use of what is available fresh from the land and sea, the people of Ireland are true to this proverb. History shows that the diet of the ancient Irish included fresh fish and meat, oats, wheat, roots, seaweed, mushrooms, leeks, watercress, apples, nuts, whortleberries (a type of blueberry), strawberries, and damsons (a type of plum). All these foods are naturally abundant in Ireland, and they remain the primary elements of Irish cuisine.

THE LAND

"The people may go, but the hills remain."

—Irish proverb

If it weren't for Ireland's position on the edge of the Atlantic Ocean, the country might never have been nicknamed the Emerald Isle.

The Irish landscape is a breathtaking combination of rolling green hillsides and dramatic cliffs surrounded by water.

Moist ocean winds make their first landfall on the island's mountainous west coast. Above the slopes, clouds form and release the mist and rain for which Ireland is famous. So much gentle rain keeps the land green.

Hundreds of small rivers run through the hills and mountains, twisting and turning as they flow inland to bigger rivers—such as the 240-mile Shannon, the longest river in the British Isles. In the low-lying areas that make up much of the middle part of Ireland, there are numerous *loughs* (lakes) and large, swampy peat bogs. Peat—soil heavy with decayed plant life—burns hot and slow. Peat is still burned in many Irish fireplaces as fuel for heating and cooking.

No part of the island is far from a coastline. The west coast in particular is indented with many inlets and fringed with numerous islands. Like the rivers, the inlets are a great source of fish.

THE PEOPLE

Irish people include Vikings, Normans, and the English among their ancestors. The Celts arrived in Ireland from northeastern Europe about 250 B.C. Gaelic is believed to have developed from the Celtic language. Gaelic and English are the two official languages of Ireland. *Céad Míle Fáilte,* a Celtic saying that means "a hundred thousand welcomes," has become a national slogan in Ireland.

Ireland is the birthplace of many celebrated authors, poets, and playwrights, including Jonathan Swift, George Bernard Shaw, and Samuel Beckett. Myrtle Allen, the founder of one of Ireland's four international cooking schools, wrote the *Ballymaloe Cookbook*—an acclaimed collection of old and new Irish recipes.

Irish linen, pottery, and glassware are in demand throughout the world. The art of flutemaking has also been passed down through countless generations of Irish craftspeople.

When the Republic of Ireland achieved independence from Britain in 1921, the Irish demonstrated their dislike of rulers and tyrants by minting coins with images of pigs, hens, hares, and salmon instead of presidents and kings.

THE FOOD

The potato is the food that is perhaps most often associated with the Irish. British explorers brought the potato to Ireland from Peru. According to legend, Sir Walter Raleigh planted the first potatoes in Ireland. They proved to be a rugged crop that would grow in small plots of soil. The potato's hardiness was especially fortunate for Irish Catholics in the 18th and 19th centuries. Allowed only tiny plots of land for farming by the ruling Protestants, many Irish people survived on potatoes. The failure of the potato crops in 1845 caused a harsh famine throughout Ireland, and the first wave of Irish immigration to the United States soon followed. With the immigrants came the recipes—with and without potatoes—that are most often associated with Irish cuisine, including corned beef and cabbage, Irish stew, and soda bread.

To this day, the Irish remain hearty potato eaters, and the potato is by far the most commonly eaten vegetable in Ireland. Well-known potato dishes are potato *farls*

Ireland is famed for its fine crystal, such as these pieces at the Galway crystal factory in county Donegal.

In Ireland, sheep are used for their wool as well as their meat.

(mashed potato and flour biscuits fried in bacon fat), *boxty* (potato bread that is baked or fried on a griddle), potato and leek soup, Dublin coddle (a stew of bacon, sausage, and potatoes), champ (creamed potatoes and scallions), colcannon (similar to champ but with the addition of kale or cabbage), *pratie oaten* (potato and oatmeal griddle cakes), and seafood, meat, and vegetable pies topped with potato crusts.

Fresh fish and seafood are abundant in Ireland, especially salmon, sole, scallops, and lobster. Fish is usually panfried, but might also be poached, grilled, or broiled. Irish lobster is usually boiled and served with butter, but two other Irish lobster recipes are well-known. Thackeray's lobster—cooked with a peppery mustard sauce—is named after William Makepeace Thackeray, who toured and wrote about Ireland in the 19th century. Dublin lawyer is a recipe of fresh lobster pieces cooked in cream.

SAINT PATRICK'S DAY

In Ireland, and in most countries of the world where English is spoken, March 17 holds great significance. It is a day of rejoicing for all Irish people—and many who are not Irish—in memory of St. Patrick, the patron saint of Ireland who died on that day.

Many Irish cities, such as Cobh in county Cork, are located on the coast.

BEFORE YOU BEGIN

Cooking any dish, plain or fancy, is easier and more fun if you are familiar with the utensils, terms, and ingredients used in a recipe. Some of the recipes in this book use ingredients and utensils you may not know. Therefore, *before* you start cooking any of the dishes in this book, carefully study the following lists of special utensils, terms, and ingredients. Then read through the recipe you want to try from beginning to end.

Now you are ready to shop for ingredients and to organize the cookware you will need. Once you have assembled everything, you can begin to cook. It is also very important to read *The Careful Cook* on page 44 before you start. Following these rules will make your cooking experience safe, fun, and easy.

COOKING UTENSILS

biscuit cutter – A circular cookie cutter with a basket-type handle

breadboard – A large wooden board with a smooth surface, used for kneading dough

Bundt cake pan – A round cake pan with fluted sides and a hollow center

cheesecloth – Gauzy cotton cloth used to strain liquid from food

colander – A bowl with small holes in the bottom and sides. It is used for draining liquid from solid food.

rolling pin – A heavy, cylindrical tool used for rolling out dough

slotted spoon – A spoon with small openings in its bowl. It is used to remove solid food from liquid.

soup tureen – A deep serving bowl, usually china, with two handles and a lid

COOKING TERMS

beat – To stir rapidly in a circular motion

boil – To heat a liquid over high heat until bubbles form and rise rapidly to the surface

brown – To cook food quickly with high heat so that the surface turns an even brown

core – To remove the inedible center of a fruit or vegetable *dice* – To chop food into small, squarish pieces

fold – To blend an ingredient with other ingredients by using a gentle, overturning circular motion rather than by stirring or beating

grate – To cut food into tiny pieces by rubbing it against a flat utensil with small holes in it called a grater

knead – To blend a mixture—usually dough—with the fingers to make it pliable

mince – To chop food into very tiny pieces

preheat – To allow an oven to warm up to the required temperature before putting food into it

sauté – To fry quickly in a small amount of oil or fat, stirring or turning the food often to prevent burning

sift – To put an ingredient, such as flour or sugar, through a utensil called a sifter to break up any lumps

simmer – To cook over low heat in liquid kept just below the boiling point. Bubbles may occasionally rise to the surface.

A group of pony trekkers rides through the Irish countryside.

SPECIAL INGREDIENTS

allspice – The berry of a West Indian tree, used whole or ground, whose flavor resembles a combination of cinnamon, nutmeg, and cloves

bay leaf – The dried leaf of the bay tree (also called laurel)

candied fruit – Fruits, often with rind, cooked in a heavy syrup until dry and then covered with sugar crystals

caraway seeds – The sharply flavored seed of a plant in the carrot family

chives – A member of the onion family. The thin green stalks are chopped and used as a garnish and a flavoring.

cinnamon – A spice made from the bark of a tree in the laurel family. It is available both ground and in sticks.

cloves – The dried buds of a small evergreen tree. Cloves can be used whole or ground.

consommé – A clear, meat-flavored broth, available in cans or in dried cubes

cracker meal – Very finely ground crackers

Many rivers wind through Ireland, providing much of the fish and seafood that make up an important part of the Irish diet.

garlic – An herb whose distinctive flavor is used in many dishes. Each bulb can be broken up into several small sections called cloves. Before chopping a clove of garlic, remove its papery skin.

juniper berries – The fruit of a tree in the cypress family. Ripe berries are harvested in autumn and used either whole or crushed in marinades and sauces.

kale – A vegetable with loose, curly, dark green or purple leaves. Kale is a member of the cabbage family.

marjoram – A fragrant herb belonging to the mint family. Its leaves are used fresh or dried.

mustard seed – The pungent yellow seed of the mustard plant, used to flavor food

nutmeg – A fragrant spice that is often used—either whole or ground—in desserts

parsley – A green leafy herb used as a seasoning and as a garnish

rosemary – An herb of the mint family, used dried or fresh, that has a strong, slightly bitter taste

thyme – A fragrant herb used fresh or dried to season food

vanilla sugar – White sugar flavored with ground vanilla beans.

watercress – An aquatic green plant with a peppery flavor. It is used in salads, soups, sauces, and as a garnish.

white pepper – Ground peppercorns with their hulls (outer shells) removed. White pepper is milder than black pepper.

AN IRISH MENU

The following are a few typical Irish menus. Recipes included in this book are marked with an asterisk.

Breakfast

* Pratie Oaten
* One-Skillet Farmhouse-Style Fry

* Soda Bread
  Butter and Marmalade

Lunch

  Menu #1
* Irish Stew
* Soda Bread
  Butter and Cheese

  Menu #2
* Dublin Coddle
* Iced Beet Salad
  Hot Rolls and Butter

Afternoon Tea

* Tea
* Wheaten Rhubarb Crumble

* Spiced Apple Tarts
* Minanollag Fruitcake

Dinner

Menu #1
* Watercress Soup
* Limerick Ham
* Sweet-and-Sour Brussels Sprouts
* Colcannon

Menu #3
* Corned Beef and Cabbage
* Boxty Bread
  Fresh Fruit Salad

Menu #2
* Nore Salmon Cakes with
    Lemon Parsley Sauce
* Champ
  Green Salad

Menu #4
* Chicken and Leek Pie
  Steamed Carrots
* Chicory Salad with
    Buttermilk-Egg Dressing
  Cheese and Crackers

For a hearty Irish breakfast, try cooking a farmhouse-style fry (center, recipe on page 21) along with pratie oaten (right, recipe on page 20) and soda bread (left).

BREAKFAST

In the Emerald Isle many people like a "good fry" to start the day. Farmers usually eat breakfast early. Irish breakfasts are substantial meals, planned to see people through the day with the help of only a light lunch. City dwellers may choose lighter fare that is quicker to prepare, such as fruit, porridge, or sliced brown bread spread with butter and marmalade.

Soda Bread

Soda bread is a nutritious bread that is simple to make. In parts of county Cork, in southern Ireland, soda bread is still cooked the old-fashioned way in a bastable oven (a heavy-lidded iron pot) suspended over a peat fire.

2 cups whole wheat flour
2 cups white flour
1 teaspoon salt
1½ teaspoons baking soda
1¾ cups buttermilk

1. Preheat oven to 375°F.
2. Sift both flours into a large bowl. Add salt and baking soda. Use both hands to scoop up dry ingredients, then open up fingers to allow mixture to drop back into the bowl. Repeat several times to help add air to the mixture.
3. Add buttermilk. Using your hands, quickly knead into a soft dough. If dough becomes too soft and sticky, add a little more flour, but work very quickly. With wet hands, shape dough into a round loaf. Smooth out wrinkles.
4. Sprinkle a baking sheet generously with flour and place dough in the middle. Use a sharp knife to cut an X about 1 inch deep on top of the loaf.
5. Place baking sheet on the top shelf of the oven. Bake for about 40 minutes or until golden brown.
6. Remove bread from oven and wrap immediately in a clean tea towel to keep crust from hardening. Allow to cool before serving.

Makes 1 loaf

Pratie Oaten

Pratie, *from the Gaelic word* prataí, *means "potato." Pratie oaten are small, fried cakes, popular at breakfast. Pratie oaten are also traditionally served at tea time in county Donegal, where the most potatoes are grown.*

2 large potatoes, peeled, washed, and cut into quarters
1 teaspoon salt
4 tablespoons butter
¾ cup stone-ground oat bran
   oil, butter, or margarine for frying

1. Preheat oven to 250°F.
2. Place potatoes in a medium-sized saucepan. Add one teaspoon of salt and enough water to cover. Bring to a boil, reduce heat to medium, cover, and cook for 15–20 minutes or until tender when pierced with a fork.
3. Drain potatoes in a colander and then pour into a medium-sized bowl. Mash well, using a potato masher. While allowing potatoes to cool, heat butter in a small saucepan over low heat until melted.
4. Sprinkle oat bran over potatoes. Add melted butter and blend well with a fork.
5. When mixture is well blended, use both hands to knead into a pliable dough. Form mixture into a round ball. Cover the dough with a clean dish towel and keep in the refrigerator until needed.
6. Place dough on a floured breadboard. Using a floured rolling pin, gently roll dough into a circle about 8 inches in diameter and 1 inch thick.
7. Use a round biscuit cutter to cut 4 circles out of the dough. Gather remaining dough into a ball, roll again, and cut out 2 more circles.
8. Heat 1 tablespoon oil, butter, or margarine in a large skillet over medium heat. Fry praties about 5 minutes on each side, or until golden brown.
9. Remove to an ovenproof serving platter. Keep praties warm in preheated oven.

Makes 6 pieces

One-Skillet Farmhouse-Style Fry

Irish bacon, which ranks among the best in the world, contains far more meat than American bacon. In the United States, Irish bacon comes in cans.

8 slices bacon
2 tomatoes, each sliced into 4 rounds
   dash of salt and pepper
8 mushrooms, washed and sliced
4 eggs

1. Preheat oven to 250°F. If you have made pratie oatens, you can use the same ovenproof platter to hold your one-skillet fry. Otherwise, place a large, ovenproof platter in the warm oven.
2. Place bacon in a large skillet and turn heat to medium. Cook until crisp. Remove the bacon from the pan, drain it on a plate lined with paper towels, and place it on the platter in oven.
3. Return skillet (with bacon fat still in it) to heat. Add tomatoes, sprinkle with salt and pepper, and fry for about 5 minutes on each side. Remove and add to platter in oven.
4. Return skillet to heat. Add mushrooms, sprinkle with salt and pepper and sauté for 5–10 minutes. Remove and add to platter in oven.
5. Gently break eggs into skillet, being careful not to break the yolks. Return skillet to heat. Spoon a little of the bacon fat over each egg yolk as it cooks. When egg whites have turned brown around the edges, remove skillet from heat.
6. Remove platter from oven. Gently place eggs on platter one at a time and serve.

Serves 4

LUNCH

Hearty soups and stews are first choices for Irish lunches during the cooler months, especially for hardworking farmers. One-pot lunches are often put together the evening before, and simmer slowly overnight on a damped-down peat fire. During summer months, people prefer sandwiches. In the cities, many establishments serve what has become known as pub grub—anything from soup and salad to a plate of sandwiches.

Dublin Coddle

Before the 18th century, this beloved one-pot dish was made with only leeks, oatmeal, and homemade pork sausages. Today it is also prepared with potatoes, onions, and chunks of ham.

4 slices bacon, cut into 1-inch pieces
1½ cups smoked ham or smoked sausage, cubed
4 potatoes, peeled, washed, and sliced into thin rounds
salt and pepper to taste
½ teaspoon dried marjoram
4 green onions, chopped

1. Preheat oven to 375°F.
2. In large nonstick skillet, fry bacon until crisp. Remove and drain on a plate lined with paper towels. Place bacon pieces in a large ovenproof casserole dish. Top with cubed ham or sausage.
3. Remove all but 1 tablespoon of the bacon fat from the skillet. Add potatoes and return to heat. Brown potatoes lightly over medium heat. The potatoes will take on the bacon flavor.
4. Place potatoes on top of ham and sprinkle well with salt and pepper. Add marjoram.
5. Add half the green parts of the onions and all the white parts. Save the remaining green parts. Pour enough water over skillet mixture to cover.
6. Cover with lid and bake for about 45 minutes, or until potatoes are tender when pierced with a fork. Remove, sprinkle with remaining green onion, and serve.

Serves 4

Iced Beet Salad

1 16-ounce can sliced beets
¼ cup white onion, minced
½ teaspoon salt
¼ teaspoon pepper
4 tablespoons apple cider vinegar
2 tablespoons chives, chopped
¼ cup sour cream

1. Pour beets into a colander and drain well. Place in a medium-sized bowl. Add onions, salt, pepper, vinegar, and half the chives. Mix well, cover with plastic wrap, and chill in refrigerator for at least 4 hours.

2. Remove from refrigerator and drain off excess liquid. Add sour cream and stir well. Top with remaining chives and serve.

Serves 4

Dublin coddle combines the Irish staples of potatoes, bacon, and ham. Creamy iced beet salad is a delicious accompaniment.

Irish Stew

The original Irish stew recipes called for goat meat. Many years ago, lambs were more valuable for their wool than for their meat. In modern stew recipes, however, lamb is widely used. Recipes vary from county to county (and family to family). Some recipes call for barley as a thickener, some call for carrots for a sweeter flavor, while others include rutabagas, known in Ireland as purple or Swedish turnips.

4 **potatoes, peeled, washed, and cubed**
4 **carrots, peeled, washed, and cut into chunks**
2 **yellow onions, peeled and cut into ¼-inch slices**
   salt and pepper to taste
3 **pounds lean boneless lamb (neck or shoulder), cut into 1-inch cubes**
½ **teaspoon dried thyme**
¼ **teaspoon dried rosemary**

1. Spread half the potatoes on the bottom of a large pan. Cover potatoes with half of the carrots and onions. Sprinkle with salt and pepper. Add all of the lamb.
2. Sprinkle the thyme and rosemary over the meat. Arrange remaining onions over the meat. Finally, top with the rest of the carrots and potatoes. Sprinkle with salt and pepper.
3. Pour in enough cold water to cover potatoes plus 1 extra inch. Bring to a boil over high heat. Reduce heat to low, cover pan, and allow stew to simmer for about 1 hour and 30 minutes, or until meat is tender.
4. Before serving Irish stew, stir well and season with more salt and pepper if necessary.

Serves 4 to 6

Carrots, onions, potatoes, and lamb combine to make an Irish lunchtime favorite—Irish stew.

AFTERNOON TEA

Afternoon tea can be a light snack between lunch and dinner, or it can be the main evening meal. Some workers returning home after a hard day's labor will sit down to a cooked meal. This will be followed by desserts such as scones (sweet biscuits) or *barm brack* (a yeasty raisin bread), both served with butter and preserves. Some city restaurants serve tea with fruit tarts, tea cakes, and a variety of finger sandwiches.

Preparing a Pot of Tea the Irish Way

1. Put a kettle of fresh water on the stove and bring to a boil.
2. Warm a china or silver teapot by filling it with hot water.
3. When water on stove boils, empty teapot, wipe excess moisture from the inside of the pot, and add loose Irish breakfast tea to pot (one teaspoonful per person, plus one extra "for the pot").

Pour boiling water over the tea, estimating two cups of tea per person plus one for the pot.
4. Cover teapot with tea cozy (a teapot cover with slits for handle and spout) and let stand for three minutes. If you don't have a tea cozy, you can wrap the teapot in a clean dish towel.
5. If you like milk in your tea, add milk to cup before pouring in the tea. After pouring tea, stir in sugar or honey to taste.
6. For extra cups of tea, add a small amount of boiling water to the pot, although brewed tea that is more than 10 or 15 minutes old tends to become bitter.

Wheaten Rhubarb Crumble

Blackberries, strawberries, and blueberries are also delicious in a crumble.

1 20-ounce package frozen rhubarb
2 tablespoons white sugar
½ cup unsalted butter

1¾ cups whole wheat flour, sifted
¼ cup rolled oats
½ cup brown sugar

1. Preheat oven to 350°F.
2. Remove frozen rhubarb from package and place in a medium-sized bowl. Add white sugar, mix well, and set aside.
3. With a sharp knife, cut butter into small pieces (this is easier to do if the butter is frozen). Pour flour into a large bowl. Using your fingertips, blend butter pieces lightly into the flour. When the mixture feels like fine bread crumbs, add the oats and the brown sugar. Mix well.
4. Place rhubarb mixture into a lightly greased 8-inch glass pie pan.
5. Sprinkle flour mixture evenly over rhubarb. Use your hands to press it down lightly and smooth out the top.
6. Bake for 45 minutes.
7. Serve the crumble warm in individual glass serving dishes. Top with cream or ice cream if desired.

Serves 6

These dainty tarts—filled with apples, nuts, and spices—add a cheerful touch to an afternoon tea party. (Recipe is on page 28.)

Spiced Apple Tarts

1 1-pound package pastry sheets (found in frozen foods section of the supermarket)
 white flour
2 apples, peeled, cored, cut into quarters, and thinly sliced
4 tablespoons white sugar
4 tablespoons ground walnuts
4 tablespoons raisins
2 tablespoons orange marmalade
⅛ teaspoon cinnamon
⅛ teaspoon nutmeg
1 egg yolk, beaten with 1 tablespoon water

1. Cut 4 shamrock patterns from a piece of 8½- by 11-inch paper. Each pattern should be about 3 inches in diameter.
2. Preheat oven to 375°F.
3. Lightly grease 4 tart pans (4½ inches in diameter by 1¼ inches deep).
4. Remove 2 pastry sheets from their inner wrapping and thaw at room temperature for 30 minutes.
5. Place thawed pastry on a floured surface and use a floured rolling pin to gently roll each sheet out to a 12-inch square.
6. Turn tart pans upside down on pastry sheets. With a sharp knife, cut around the outside of each pan, leaving a ¾-inch border
7. Place the tart pans on the other pastry sheet. Cut 4 more disks, but this time cut flush with the edges of the tart pans.

8. Gather the remaining dough and knead it together lightly. Roll out a sheet large enough to hold the 4 shamrocks. Place the paper patterns on dough and cut around them with a sharp knife. Set aside.

9. In a medium-sized bowl, mix together apples, sugar, nuts, raisins, marmalade, cinnamon, and nutmeg.

10. Turn tart pans right side up and set them on a large baking sheet. Place 1 large dough disk in each pan. Using your fingers, shape dough around top edges of pans to form a border. Fill each shell with equal amounts of the apple mixture.

11. With a pastry brush or a damp paper towel, brush the egg yolk around the top edges of tarts. Top each tart with a small dough disk. Use the back of a fork to seal the edges. Brush a little more egg yolk over the tops and then place a shamrock shape in the middle of each tart. Brush again with egg yolk. With a sharp knife, cut 4 small slits into the dough around the shamrock.

12. Bake for 25 minutes or until golden brown. Cool before serving. (For a

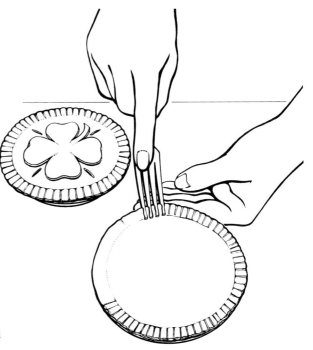

festive appearance, outline the shamrocks using a squeeze tube of prepared green icing.)

Makes 4 tarts

Irish tea is usually served with tempting sweets, such as Minanollag fruitcake (left) and wheaten rhubarb crumble (right, recipe on page 26).

Minanollag Fruitcake

Minanollag *means "December" in Gaelic. These rich cakes grace many Irish tables during the Christmas season.*

shortening and flour for preparing pan
½ **cup unsalted butter or margarine, cut into small pieces and softened**
3 **eggs, separated**
1½ **cups brown sugar**
1 **teaspoon vanilla sugar**
1 **teaspoon allspice**
1 **tablespoon cinnamon**
⅛ **teaspoon nutmeg**
1 **cup white flour**
1 **cup whole wheat flour**
1½ **tablespoons baking powder**
¾ **cup milk**
¾ **cup raisins**
1 **cup mixed candied fruit, finely chopped**
¼ **cup walnuts, chopped**
¾ **cup carrots, shredded**

1. Preheat oven to 375°F.
2. Grease and lightly flour a Bundt cake pan.
3. Place butter, egg yolks, brown sugar, vanilla sugar, allspice, cinnamon, and nutmeg in a large bowl and mix well.
4. Sift both flours and baking powder on top of mixture. Stir well, adding a little milk if needed to keep the mixture smooth. Stirring constantly, add raisins, candied fruit, nuts, carrots, and the remaining milk.
5. With a hand mixer, beat egg whites until stiff peaks form. Carefully fold egg whites into batter and pour into prepared Bundt cake pan.
6. Bake for 50 minutes to 1 hour, or until toothpick inserted into cake comes out clean.
7. When cake has cooled slightly, invert pan onto a large round cake plate. When completely cool, dust whole cake with powdered sugar, then slice and serve.

Makes 12 slices

DINNER

For those Irish people who have a light afternoon tea, dinner is the largest meal of the day, eaten between 7:00 and 9:00 P.M. For those who eat a substantial meal in the afternoon, dinner is a light meal. In elegant city restaurants, menus might include appetizers, hot or cold soup, a fish course, a main dish served with a green salad, dessert, and finally crackers and cheese.

Watercress Soup

Watercress has a peppery flavor. When combined with potatoes and cream, it lends itself to a nutritious hot or cold soup.

1 tablespoon unsalted butter
1 large green onion, chopped
4 potatoes, peeled, washed, and cubed
2 tablespoons white flour
½ teaspoon salt
dash of white pepper
1 14½ ounce can chicken consommé or leftover chicken stock
2 cups watercress, washed and finely chopped
1 cup milk
¾ cup light cream

1. Melt butter in a large pan over medium heat. Add white parts of onion and the potatoes and sauté for about 5 minutes, stirring several times.
2. Sprinkle flour, salt, and pepper over mixture, blending well. Add chicken stock a little at a time, stirring continuously until all chicken stock has been added.
3. Cover pan, turn heat to medium low, and allow mixture to simmer for 25 minutes or until potatoes are very tender. Remove from heat and mash well.
4. Return pan to heat. Add watercress, green onion tops, and milk. Simmer for 20 minutes.
5. Pour soup into a large soup tureen. Add cream, and salt or pepper according to taste. Serve immediately. (This soup may also be served cold.)

Serves 4

Chicken and Leek Pie

1 package ready-made pie crust (found in the freezer section of the grocery store)
6 slices of lean bacon, chopped
2 small leeks, chopped
4 boneless chicken breasts, cooked and cut into bite-sized pieces (about 1½ cups)
6 tablespoons white flour
½ teaspoon dried rosemary
¼ teaspoon salt
½ teaspoon pepper
4 tablespoons milk or half and half
½ cup sour cream
2 tablespoons parsley, chopped
4 tablespoons milk for glazing

1. Preheat oven to 400°F.
2. Press 1 ready-made pie crust into a 9-inch round pie pan or baking dish. Trim any extra dough around edges.
3. In a large skillet over medium-high heat, fry the bacon until crisp. Remove to a platter lined with paper towels. Remove skillet from heat. Save bacon grease.
4. Place leeks and chicken pieces in a plastic bag. Add flour. Twist the top of the bag (making sure it is securely closed) and shake well to coat leeks and chicken with flour.
5. Add the flour-coated pieces to bacon grease in skillet. Discard any leftover flour. Sauté over medium-high heat until leeks and chicken pieces are lightly browned, stirring constantly. Remove from heat.
6. Stir in bacon, rosemary, salt, pepper, milk, and sour cream. Blend well.
7. Place mixture in pie shell. Sprinkle with parsley. Top with second ready-made pie crust. Press edges together with fingers and seal with the back of a fork.
8. With a pastry brush or a damp paper towel, brush top of pie with milk. Make several slits in the center of the dough (this allows steam to escape). Bake for 20 minutes. Reduce heat to 350° and bake for another 15 to 20 minutes, until crust is a light golden brown.

Serves 4

A mixture of brown sugar, apple juice, and ju-niper berries gives Limerick ham with sweet-and-sour brussels sprouts its special flavor. Colcannon (recipe on page 38) is a potato dish traditionally eaten on Halloween.

Limerick Ham with Sweet-and-Sour Brussels Sprouts

The special flavor of Limerick ham comes from juniper bush branches used in the smoking process. Juniper grows freely in county Limerick. This recipe dates back to the 18th century. You can use leftovers for Dublin coddle.

 1 8–10 pound smoked ham (with
    bone)
¾ cup brown sugar
¼ teaspoon ground cloves
¼ cup cracker meal
 4 cups apple juice
12 whole dried juniper berries

1. Preheat oven to 400°F.
2. With a sharp knife, carefully remove thick skin from ham.
3. In a medium-sized bowl, mix together brown sugar, cloves, and cracker meal.
4. Place ham in the middle of large baking pan (a turkey pan works well).

Using your hands, carefully pack brown sugar mixture in a thick layer on the top and around the sides of the ham. Pour 3 cups of the apple juice around the ham and add the juniper berries.

5. Cover and bake for about 3½ hours (20 minutes for each pound), adding remaining apple juice about halfway through cooking time to keep ham from drying out.

6. Slice ham and arrange slices on a serving platter.

Serves 4

Sweet-and-Sour Brussels Sprouts

These brussels sprouts are cooked along with the Limerick ham, acquiring both the delicious flavor of the ham's juices and the brown-sugar crust that coats the meat. For a more colorful meal, add chopped carrots along with the sprouts.

24 fresh brussels sprouts, or
    2 10-ounce boxes frozen
1 teaspoon salt
¼ teaspoon white pepper

1. If you are using fresh brussels sprouts, peel away the outer leaves, cut off bottom stems, and wash well. Place sprouts around the ham 40 minutes before it is done baking. If using frozen sprouts, thaw according to package directions and add to ham 15 minutes before ham is done.

2. When the ham is done, use a slotted spoon to remove the brussels sprouts (and carrots if used). Arrange sprouts around ham before serving. Spoon a little juice from the pan over ham and sprouts.

Serves 4

Nore Salmon Cakes with Lemon Parsley Sauce

1 14¾ ounce can pink salmon
½ cup cracker meal, mashed potatoes, or raw potatoes peeled, washed, and finely grated
1 egg, beaten
4 tablespoons fresh parsley, washed and finely chopped
¼ cup lemon parsley sauce (Recipe follows.)
1 tablespoon freshly squeezed lemon juice
¼ teaspoon pepper
   oil for frying

1. Open can of salmon and drain off all liquid. Place in a large bowl and remove the larger bones from salmon using a fork.
2. Add cracker meal, mashed or grated potatoes, egg, parsley, lemon parsley sauce, lemon juice, and pepper. Mix well.
3. Heat 2 tablespoons of oil in a large frying pan over medium heat. Scoop out salmon mixture using a soup spoon and shape with wet hands into round flat cakes.
4. Fry cakes for about 5 minutes on each side or until they are an even golden brown.
5. Remove to a serving plate. Top each salmon cake with a heaping spoonful of lemon parsley sauce before serving.

Makes 8–10 cakes

Lemon Parsley Sauce

3 tablespoons fresh parsley, washed and finely chopped
1 tablespoon lemon juice
1 teaspoon grated lemon peel
1 cup mayonnaise
⅛ teaspoon salt
⅛ teaspoon white pepper
1 tablespoon milk or light cream

1. Place all ingredients into a food processor or blender and process until sauce is smooth and flecked with green.

Makes 1 cup of sauce

Named after the salmon-filled Nore River, tasty Nore salmon cakes are served with lemon parsley sauce and accompanied by champ (left, recipe on page 39) and a green salad.

Colcannon

Traditionally eaten on Halloween, colcannon is made with creamed potatoes and either leeks, kale, or cabbage, depending on the region of the country that the recipe comes from. Colcannon comes with a tradition: several tokens or favors are hidden in the colcannon, such as a gold ring, a sixpence (similar to a dime), a thimble, or a button. Superstition has it that if you get the ring you will be married within a year, and if you get the sixpence you will become wealthy. If you get the thimble or the button, you'll remain unmarried.

1 tablespoon butter or margarine
3 cups kale, washed and finely chopped
2 tablespoons white onion, finely chopped
¼ cup water
4 potatoes, peeled, washed, and cubed
¼ cup milk

½ teaspoon salt
¼ teaspoon pepper

1. Heat a large skillet over medium heat and add the butter. When the butter is melted, sauté kale and onion for about 5 minutes, stirring frequently. Add the water, turn heat to medium-low, cover, and simmer for 20 minutes.
2. Place potatoes in a medium-sized saucepan, cover with water, and cook over medium heat until tender (about 20 minutes).
3. Remove potato pan from heat. Drain potatoes into a colander, then place them in a large bowl and mash well with a potato masher while adding the milk.
4. Remove kale from heat and drain off excess liquid. Add kale mixture to potato mixture. Sprinkle in the salt and pepper and blend well. Serve immediately.

Serves 4

Champ

Champ is similar to colcannon. Cooks who live along the Irish seacoasts sometimes add dulse (edible seaweed) to their champ.

4 large potatoes, peeled, washed, and cubed
4 green onions, chopped
¾ cup milk
2 tablespoons butter
1 teaspoon salt
½ teaspoon white pepper

1. Place potatoes in a medium-sized saucepan, cover with water, and cook over medium heat until tender when pierced with a fork (about 20 minutes).
2. While the potatoes cook, place all the white parts and half the green parts of the onions into a small saucepan. Add milk. Simmer over medium-low heat for 5–10 minutes. Remove from heat.
3. Drain potatoes into a colander and then place them in a large bowl. Mash well with a potato masher, adding onion mixture, butter, salt, and pepper. Sprinkle with remaining onion tops and serve. You can make a well in the center of the champ and fill it with melted butter or scrambled eggs.

Serves 4

Corned beef and cabbage are simmered together for a hearty main dish, served with boxty bread (left, recipe on page 42) and a salad of fresh fruit.

Corned Beef and Cabbage

In the United States, corned beef boiled with cabbage has been associated with Ireland since the first large wave of Irish immigration to the United States in the 19th century. Corned beef is also called salt beef because it is rubbed with coarse salt before being pickled in brine.

1 **tablespoon vegetable oil**
1 **large white onion, cut into rings**
1 **clove garlic, minced**
2 **pounds corned beef, pickled in ready-made brine**
1 **teaspoon salt**
½ **teaspoon pepper**
1 **bay leaf**
1 **teaspoon mustard seeds or pickling spice**
1 **small head green cabbage, washed, cored, and cut into quarters**

1. Heat oil in a large pot over medium heat. Sauté onion and garlic in oil until onion is golden brown. Reduce heat to low.
2. Remove corned beef from package and rinse with cold water. Blot excess water with a paper towel.
3. Using a wooden spoon, push onions and garlic to one side of the pot. Place corned beef, fatty side down, in the middle of pot. Turn heat up to medium-high. Cook for 5 minutes to brown, turn meat over and brown for 5 more minutes.
4. Add salt, pepper, bay leaf, mustard seeds, and enough water to cover meat. Turn heat to medium-low, cover, and simmer for 2½ hours.
5. Remove cover and add cabbage. Replace cover and simmer for 20 minutes. Remove from heat.
6. Remove corned beef to a large serving plate and slice into medium-sized pieces. Remove cabbage with a slotted spoon and arrange around sliced corned beef before serving.

Serves 4

Boxty Bread

The name boxty *comes from the Gaelic word* bacstaí, *which means "bread made from potato pulp."*

3 **large potatoes, peeled, washed, and cubed**
3 **large potatoes, peeled, washed, and cut into quarters**
1¾ **cup self-rising flour**
6 **tablespoons butter, melted**
½ **teaspoon salt**
½ **teaspoon baking soda**
1 **teaspoon caraway seeds**
4 **tablespoons milk**

1. Preheat oven to 300°F.
2. Place the cubed potatoes in a medium-sized saucepan, cover with water, and cook over medium heat until tender when pierced with a fork (about 20 minutes).
3. Grate the remaining potatoes using a small-holed grater. Wrap the pulp in cheesecloth and squeeze out all the water into a glass.
4. Place potato pulp in a large bowl and loosen with a fork. Mix in any potato starch that settles in the bottom of the glass of potato water.
5. Drain cooked potatoes in a colander. Return them to pan and mash well with a potato masher. Add the mashed potatoes to the raw potatoes. Sift the flour on top. With a wooden spoon, blend in 2 tablespoons of potato water, melted butter, salt, baking soda, and caraway seeds.
6. Using both hands, knead this dough well. Divide dough into 4 equal pieces. Shape each piece into a round, flat cake. Place on a well-greased baking sheet and cut an X about 1 inch deep in the top of each cake with a sharp knife.
7. With a pastry brush or a damp paper towel, brush the dough well with potato water. Bake for 35 minutes. Remove loaves from oven, brush each loaf with milk, and bake for another 5 to 7 minutes or until golden brown. Each loaf of boxty can be split into farls (quarters) and served hot with butter.

Serves 8

Chicory Salad with Buttermilk-Egg Dressing

Chicory roots are used as a coffee substitute, while the long, ragged, curly leaves are known as endive. These leaves should always be washed thoroughly in warm water to remove their slightly bitter taste.

1 **medium-sized head of endive, washed and cut into ½-inch strips**
  salt and pepper to taste
4 **tablespoons apple cider vinegar**
4 **tablespoons vegetable oil**
1 **teaspoon white sugar**
  buttermilk-egg dressing (Recipe follows.)

1. Place washed and cut endive leaves in a bowl of warm water, allow to sit for about 1 minute, and drain well in a colander.
2. Place leaves in a salad bowl. Sprinkle with salt and pepper. Add vinegar, oil, and sugar. Use salad forks to mix well.
3. Place in individual salad bowls and top each with a heaping tablespoon of buttermilk-egg dressing.

Serves 4

Buttermilk-Egg Dressing

1 **hard-boiled egg, finely chopped**
1 **tablespoon chives, chopped**
¼ **cup sour cream**
¼ **cup buttermilk**
⅛ **teaspoon white pepper**

1. In a medium-sized bowl, blend all ingredients together well with a fork.

Makes about ½ cup

THE CAREFUL COOK

Whenever you cook, you must always keep certain safety rules in mind. Even experienced cooks follow these rules when they are in the kitchen.

1. Always wash your hands before handling food.

2. Thoroughly wash all raw vegetables and fruits to remove dirt, chemicals, and pesticides.

3. Use a cutting board when cutting up vegetables and fruits. Don't cut them up in your hand! And be sure to cut away from you and your fingers.

4. Long hair or loose clothing can catch fire if brought near the burners of a stove. If you have long hair, tie it back before you start cooking.

5. Turn all pot handles away from you so that you will not catch your sleeves or jewelry on them. This is especially important when younger children are around. They could easily knock a pot off the stove and get burned.

6. Always use a pot holder to steady pots or to take pans out of the oven. Don't use a wet cloth on a hot pot because the steam it produces can burn you.

7. Lift the lid of a steaming pot with the opening away from you so that you will not get burned by the steam.

8. If you get burned, hold the burn under cold running water. Do not put grease or butter on the burn. Cold water helps take the heat out, but grease or butter will only keep it in.

9. If grease or cooking oil catches fire, throw baking soda or salt at the bottom of the flame to put it out. (Water will *not* put out a grease fire.) Call for help, and try to turn all the stove burners to "off."

METRIC CONVERSION CHART

WHEN YOU KNOW		MULTIPLY BY	TO FIND	
MASS (weight)				
ounces	(oz)	28.0	grams	(g)
pounds	(lb)	0.45	kilograms	(kg)
VOLUME				
teaspoons	(tsp)	5.0	milliliters	(ml)
tablespoons	(Tbsp)	15.0	milliliters	
fluid ounces	(oz)	30.0	milliliters	
cup	(c)	0.24	liters	(l)
pint	(pt)	0.47	liters	
quart	(qt)	0.95	liters	
gallon	(gal)	3.8	liters	
TEMPERATURE				
Fahrenheit	(°F)	5/9 (after subtracting 32)	Celsius	(°C)

COMMON MEASURES AND THEIR EQUIVALENTS

3 teaspoons = 1 tablespoon

8 tablespoons = 1/2 cup

2 cups = 1 pint

2 pints = 1 quart

4 quarts = 1 gallon

16 ounces = 1 pound

INDEX

(recipes indicated by **boldface** type)

ABOUT THE AUTHOR

Helga Hughes received her early culinary training at a private college in Forcheim, Bavaria. After moving to the United States, she wrote cooking articles for national newspapers and magazines, and books on Austrian and vegetarian cooking. When not in the kitchen, Hughes follows her other writing interests—exercise and children—and promotes her books.